Red and Green Choices

Written by : Shabana Ahmed
Illustrated by : Esti Wibawati

Red and Green Choices

December 2024

Story copyright Shabana Ahmed
Illustration copyright Esti Wibawati

For my sweet grandchildren,
Faris and Manha
May Allah SWT always guide you
to make green choices!

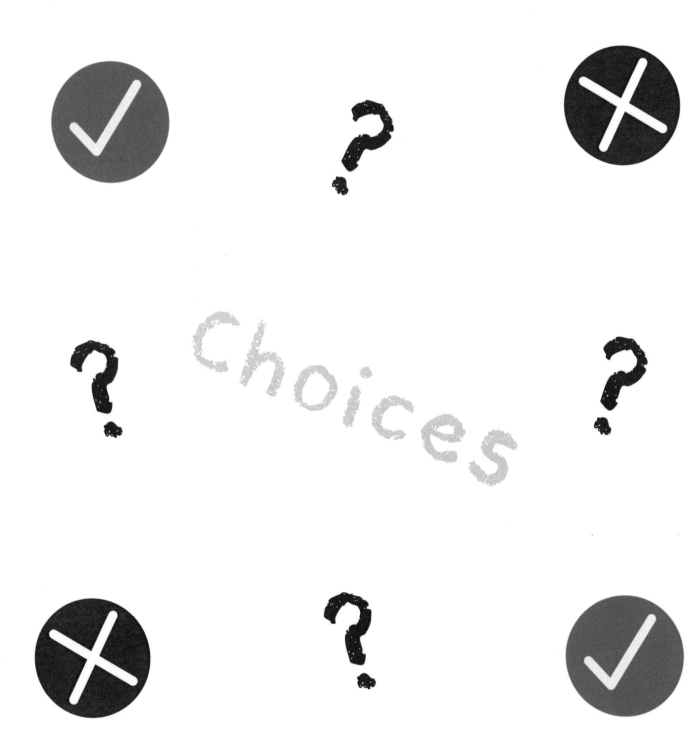

Let's start with...

Bismillah

In the name of Allah

A long time ago, where the stars sparkle bright,

Angels and jinns were created with Allah's might.

1

The angels, obeyed all HIS
commands with grace,

They bowed down to HIM,
in a beautiful place.

The jinns however,
were being tested,

To see who obeyed
and who protested.

3

Then one day, to all
Allah swt announced,

The creation of humans,
which one jinn denounced!

Humans will be my best creation
Allah swt had declared.

"But I am the best!"
that jinn thought.
His thoughts were impaired!

The angels and jinns were
commanded to prostrate
to Adam,
the first human created.

All obeyed and did
as they were told,
but this command of Allah,
that jinn negated!

6

I am made from smokeless fire and the human just from clay!

Shaytan was the name of that jinn and that is what he had to say!

"I'll make the humans disobey
you, Almighty Allah!" he said.

Not being ashamed
of what he did,
he was being rebellious instead!

8

Whoever follows you,
Allah swt said
to the rebellious one,

Will go to hell with you
and justice will surely be done!

Whoever follows my command
will however earn,

In paradise,an eternal,
beautiful life in return!

10

So that's why we hear in our head, two voices,

and that's why we always have two choices!

11

Bad choices are RED choices
from Shaytan, which will make
us land,

In a fire with him,
which   we   won't   be   able   to
withstand!

12

When we follow Allah's
command and make
GREEN choices,
our mistakes HE will pardon,

And forever grant us a life,
in the BEST paradise garden!

13

Do you know which choices are RED and which are GREEN?

Hitting

Smiling

Obeying your parents

Sharing

15

Lying

Yelling

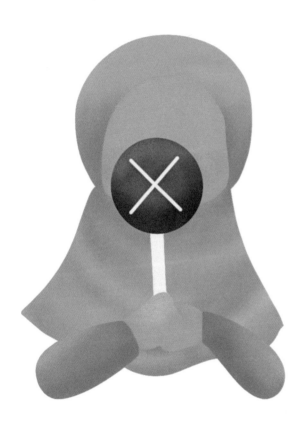

Remember to always make GREEN choices,
Don't listen to the red choice voices!
But if you do make a mistake,
quickly change your way.
For Allah swt loves to forgive
and He loves the ones who obey!

Anas bin Malik narrated that the Messenger of Allah (pbuh) said:
"Whoever asks Allah (swt) for Paradise three times, Paradise says: 'O Allah, admit him into Paradise', and whoever seeks refuge from the Fire three times, the Fire says: 'O Allah, save him from the Fire.'

Jami' at-Tirmidhi 2572

18

اللَّهُمَّ أَجِرْنِي مِنَ النَّارِ

Oh Allah, protect me from the hellfire

اللَّهُمَّ أَجِرْنِي مِنَ النَّارِ

Oh Allah, protect me from the hellfire

اللَّهُمَّ أَجِرْنِي مِنَ النَّارِ

Oh Allah, protect me from the hellfire

19

اللَّهُمَّ إِنِّي أَسْأَلُكَ الْجَنَّةَ

O Allah, I ask you for Jannah

اللَّهُمَّ إِنِّي أَسْأَلُكَ الْجَنَّةَ

O Allah, I ask you for Jannah

اللَّهُمَّ إِنِّي أَسْأَلُكَ الْجَنَّةَ

O Allah, I ask you for Jannah

Let's end with...

Alhumdulillah

All praise be to Allah

About the Author

Shabana Ahmed is a teaching wizard with two decades of experience up her sleeve! Nestled in Alpharetta, Georgia, she's on a mission to sprinkle the magic of reading, writing, and learning onto young minds. When she's not busy crafting tales for kiddos, you can find her conquering hiking trails, getting crafty, dabbling in graphic design, or having a blast with her two adorable grandkids. Shabana's creativity and passion for learning light up everything she touches, turning her books into delightful adventures for readers of all ages!

About the Illustrator

Esti Wibawati is a mom who loves art, especially drawing and painting. She started to illustrate children's books in late 2019 and has illustrated several books since then, including 2 of her own. As she grew up in Indonesia, she was used to seeing Islamic resources everywhere, however, when she moved to the States she found it hard to find simple reminder posters for her kids. That realization led her to create her small business that focuses on creating Islamic merch. Say hi to her through her Instagram @mba_esh.

Made in the USA
Las Vegas, NV
09 January 2025